Reflections of a Disgruntled American Gargoyle

Reflections of a Disgruntled American Gargoyle

Allen R. Remaley

authorHOUSE®

AuthorHouse™
1663 Liberty Drive
Bloomington, IN 47403
www.authorhouse.com
Phone: 1 (800) 839-8640

Published by AuthorHouse 05/18/2016

ISBN: 978-1-5246-0781-4 (sc)
ISBN: 978-1-5246-0780-7 (e)

Library of Congress Control Number: 2016907994

Print information available on the last page.

Dedication

To: That nebulous silent majority, wherever you are.

Special thanks to Mack Hawthorne for the cover design.

Reflections of a Disgruntled American Gargoyle

Yep! That's me. I'm out of place, out of sync and at odds with that which is taking place in my country. Like others my age, older than dirt, it strikes me that what once was good is now considered passé. So, here we go. Tag along and let's take a stroll over some familiar paths.

For those of us lucky enough to have visited or lived in the City of Light, it is more than likely that you paid a visit to Notre Dame Cathedral. If you didn't, you are in a distinct minority of the world's travelers. Nothing wrong with that; you just passed up an opportunity to have reached out and touched eight hundred years of history.

Like millions who have trekked along Parisian paths trodden by tribal groups, Romans, Goths, Vikings, occupying forces and victors, your footsteps ultimately lead toward one of the world's greatest monuments---Notre Dame Cathedral. Its portals, admired over the last eight hundred years, portray an array of sculptures depicting the greatest moments of Christianity. Once inside this magnificent edifice, your gaze is automatically drawn to the marvelous stained-glass windows used as teaching tools for medieval church goers whose Latin or French reading skills were lacking. The stories told in those pieces of colored glass still hold one's gaze, and if you listen carefully, you can imagine in your mind's eye and ear a hooded monk instructing a flock of believers about Christian saints. Those same windows were once viewed with awe by Joan of Arc, Mary Queen of Scots, Napoleon Bonaparte, Charles De Gaulle and yes, thousands of Americans. But, the real stuff, things most visitors never see, is locked away in vaults or higher up in the upper levels of the church.

Every Easter Sunday, Notre Dame opens up its vault to the public. There, collected by Louis IX, Saint Louis, on one of his crusades to the Holy Land, rests the relics of the church. Among them is what is rumored to be the original crown of thorns of Jesus Christ. My guess is that some Muslim Arab made a killing in a Jerusalem market place when the French king passed by. The crown was at one time located in La Sainte Chappelle, a church built by Saint Louis especially to hold relics accumulated during his jaunts to the Holy Land. But, there is more to the church in which Napoleon was crowned Emperor.

If you are lucky enough to visit the church when one of the attendants is in charge of the belfry tower nearest the Seine, then, for the price of entry, you will be able to climb the winding stone stairway to the second stage of the cathedral. That climb is not without some degree of courage and strength. The winding stairway is narrow, and those who made the climb early must use the same path to the bottom. You must squeeze by passersby as you ascend, and you are close enough to those descending to determine what they might have consumed for lunch. Surefootedness does help while you are in the passage way, and the only light is that which passes in from the outside of the stone walkway through little slits in the structure. But, the climb is worth the effort.

Once you reach the lofty heights of the second stage of the cathedral, i.e., after working your way up the narrow passage way and avoiding those coming down the same stairway after their own climb, you find yourself looking down into the plaza in front of the church. Using your imagination, you can almost hear the multitudes cursing Quasimodo when he claimed sanctuary in Hugo's novel which, by the way, is not entitled "The Hunchback of Notre Dame". Hugo's masterpiece is entitled <u>Notre Dame de Paris</u>, and the main character of the novel is not Quasimodo. It is the church itself. When Hugo penned the novel in 1830, the cathedral was in very poor condition. Napoleon had used the church to stable his horses. Hugo called attention to the church, and almost immediately, Parisians participated in a movement to renovate the edifice. Thanks to a novel, we are able to enjoy its sights and sounds.

Standing near the front wall, visitors look down upon what seem to be Monopoly pieces. *Bateaux mouches* ply the Seine while those on board the tourists boats look up at the majesty of the cathedral. Barges tied up to the quays along the river serve as houseboats, and the statue of Charlemagne stands guard near the river's banks as the flotilla passes by. And, there is more to see just close at hand.

If you find yourself standing on the second-level platform of the cathedral, look around closely for an attendant wearing the blue uniform of a public worker. If you stumble upon such a person, ask him or her if he or she would show you the *Grosse Marie*, the huge bell which, in Hugo's novel, Quasimodo rode as he rang out the chimes of the church. The writer explains how his character lost his hearing because of such antics.

The bell itself is enormous. Its mouth could shelter thirty people from the sun or from a rain storm. On one of my tours with high school students, the entire group of forty managed to squeeze together under Marie's shadow. Fortunately, no one rang the bell, and most of us still have our hearing intact. As you move to the front of the platform and its overlook, there is still more to see.

Observing the crowds of people below, as they have done for eight hundred years, are the massive stone statues called Gargoyles. Created by the medieval builders of the cathedral, these silent sentinels act as guardians in at least two ways. Some of these stone creatures have groves running along their backs which serve as troughs. These channels rid the stone façade of the cathedral of rain water which, if left uncontrolled, would erode the stone surface of the church. The second reason why the Gargoyles remain at their posts has to do with that which the twelfth-century stone masons and church builders needed; these awesome-looking half-human, half-animal likenesses were meant to ward off evil spirits. But, they seem, to some, to be more human than animal.

In their solid inanimate state, they look down upon the public below. They are unable to find fault with or criticize the goings-on of the millions of visitors who have passed beneath their gaze. They cannot judge, and remained silent when the Vikings ransacked Paris. They were unable to complain when hundreds of eighteenth-century prisoners were paraded before the church on their way to the guillotine during the Revolution. They looked down on Napoleon's horses as they were led inside the cathedral then used as a stable, and these solid-state monsters were unable to shed tears of shame when Hitler's soldiers paraded in front of the cathedral. No spittle rained from their mouths down on the Nazi troops below. When De Gaulle walked into the cathedral on the day Paris was liberated from the Germans, no words of thanks were uttered from mouths sealed in stone. Those majestic motionless monsters must have felt the frustration of centuries, and if these Gargoyles were able to express themselves, what a legacy they might have left. In my own way, a certain feeling of loss makes me sorry that certain stories have not been told. I, too, from time to time, feel frustrated that things are left unsaid. In our times of political correctness, racial bias, social mores and the power of the media, our thoughts and opinions are muted. It is my intention to give voice to the Gargoyle inside me. Let us begin.

Black Lives Matter?

At the moment of this jotting down of things which come to mind, the American political campaigns are in full swing. Republicans and Democrats put their candidates for the presidency on display. Supporters contribute small and large sums of money in an effort to sway opinion as to who should replace Barack Obama as President of the United States. Let me make an effort to be objective.

My votes did not go toward electing the first black-American President. In my lifetime, nothing comes to mind which would indicate that my vote was based on race. My family records can be traced back to 1749 when the German ship, <u>Lydia</u>, sailed from Rotterdam loaded with families who carried the names, Mueller, Helfrick, Sheaffer, and Remliech. When the ship docked somewhere in Philadelphia, indentured servants and families moved westward toward Pittsburgh and started farming. None of those families ever owned slaves; they were poor farmers and later, coal miners who struggled along with every other citizen living at the time.

Growing up in Pennsylvania, especially in the western part of the state, boys played football. On the football field in the 50's, color played no part in whether you had a teammate whose skin was one color or another. You played football, and when anyone drew blood, it was always red whether it came from a black or white American. In the Marine Corps, the man beside you in a tent or on maneuvers was a fellow Marine. You shared a tent, a foxhole and food with that person. When the young, first-term Senator from Illinois ran for President, my hopes were that he would work to make our country stronger. So far in his two-term presidency, those hopes were dashed on the rocks of what has seemed to be a prejudice voiced by the new president and his wife.

One of the first things Michelle Obama uttered on the eve of her husband's nomination was this: "This is the first time I have ever been proud of my country." Here is a woman who witnessed the good work of Martin Luther King, the rise of affirmative action, which helped her achieve on the American scene. She watched as the Berlin Wall fell because of an American President's persistence, and she had to be aware of the humanitarian efforts of her country on behalf of third-world countries. My God, woman! Where have you been? But, my disillusionment with Michelle's husband came soon after.

Before any documentation of our President's failings are cited, the world wanted to see this first black American succeed, too. Even before his first one hundred days in office, Obama was named the recipient of the Nobel Peace Prize. Many Americans wondered whether they had fallen asleep for months while this man from Illinois was working miracles. No explanation was ever brought to light which gave merit to the choice of those in Stockholm, and American media went the way of Chris Matthews, the MSNBC reporter, who claimed that Obama's finely-creased trousers sent a shiver of emotion up his back. Matthews is still enamored with his American President. My opinion of our president is not as gushy.

In the eyes of many Americans, Barack Obama has become the most divisive president in American history. Here is a man who, if he had wanted, could have united Americans to climb over the barrier of black versus white. Almost immediately, our president allowed his own prejudices to color his actions. Early in his inaugural campaign, it was brought to light that Obama had been attending a black-activist church in Chicago. That church, the Trinity United, was headed by the Reverend Jeremiah Wright, the man who was in charge of the marriage ceremony of Barack and Michelle. In 2008, Wright had criticized his country in a sermon by saying, "The chickens have come home to roost. God damn America!" Obama defended Wright's speech saying that he had been the minister's friend, and that he would not abandon that friendship. There is nothing wrong in standing by a friend, but, what our president did in the following months is worse.

On July 16, 2009, Henry Louis Gates, a Harvard professor known for his work tracing American ancestry, was arrested at his home in Cambridge. Gates had just returned to Boston from China where he had investigated the family history of Yo Yo Ma, the French-born, Chinese-American cellist. Gates, a black American, and his driver found that the door to Gates' home was jammed. The two men then tried to force the door open. A Cambridge police sergeant named James Crowley had been alerted by a neighbor that two men were trying to gain entrance to a home. Confronted by Crowley, Gates immediately became agitated and was arrested by Crowley for disturbing the peace. The next day, the President of the United States assertively inserted himself into the controversy by stating, "I don't know, not having been there, what role race played in that...but, the Cambridge police acted stupidly." Shortly thereafter, in an attempt to quell the controversy, one he had inflamed, Obama invited both Gates and Crowley to Washington where the three men engaged in a conversation while sharing a beer. This now famous "Beer Summit" was reported by the media and given approval as to how race issues were to be resolved. And, Gates, the Harvard professor, recently demanded that white Americans pay reparations to black Americans because of slavery. It does not take much imagination to realize why the professor might have incited an argument with a white police officer. Obama continued to suggest that America was a nation which "stuck to its Bible and its guns", and that, to our president, could not stand. No mention ever about Muslims sticking to the <u>Quran</u> and initiating terrorist acts came from our President. But, soon, another side of our American President was to come to light.

On November 5, 2009, Nidal Hasan, an American-born Muslim and U.S. Army major and psychiatrist, entered a Fort Hood, Texas cafeteria and shot and killed thirteen people and wounded thirty more. Federal law enforcement authorities immediately called the shooting an act of workplace violence in spite of the fact that Hasan shouted out, "Allah Akbar" as he was killing unarmed military personnel. As if to throw salt into wounds of relatives of the victims, the U.S. government declined requests from the victims' families to categorize the shooting as an act of Islamic terrorism. Hasan was sentenced to death on August 28, 2013, and he remains on death row in a federal prison. Barack Obama still refuses to call Hasan's cowardly act one of Islamic terrorism. Americans began to question the president's pro-Islamic leaning. But, there was more evidence of the American President's hesitation to point the finger of guilt at Muslims.

The year, 2012, did not bode well for Americans and their president. On February 16 of that year, George Zimmerman, a home security guard and part-time student confronted a teenager, Trayvon Martin, in a Florida-community walkway. Words were exchanged, and an argument/struggle ensued. Martin was shot and killed by Zimmerman. After an investigation took place, Zimmerman was exonerated. Riots took place in black-American communities. President Obama once again allowed himself to enter the fray on the side of the black-American teenager. In a speech condemning the public safety official findings, Obama opined to Martin's parents, "You know, if I had a son, he'd look like Trayvon." Instead of expressing a sadness for both parties, the American President could not shed his spots and call for solidarity of the American spirit. But, the smoke of the Florida riots had hardly cleared when yet another incident took place.

On August 9, 2014, in Ferguson, MO, a young black American teenager, Michael Brown, entered a convenience store run by a middle-aged American of oriental origin. Brown, over six foot tall and weighing over two hundred pounds, bullied the store owner and made off with several items without paying. All this was caught on tape and shown repeatedly to the American viewing public. Shortly after the theft, the police were called and arrived in the area of the crime.

A short distance away from the store, Michael Brown was confronted by a policeman in his patrol car. Brown and the police officer argued. It was alleged that the teenager tried to wrestle away the patrolman's weapon. Brown was shot and died in the street. One of Brown's friends then claimed that Michael had put his hands in the air and yelled, "Don't shoot!" That statement, later found to be a lie, led to a rallying cry by protesters, "Hands up. Don't shoot!" Protesters began wearing T-shirts with this logo, and they wore them in the streets while riots, looting and burning reigned for days. But, the flames in Ferguson were soon going to be fanned by others. Al Sharpton came to town.

Al Sharpton, the race baiter who supported Tawana Brawley, a young black-American teenager located in Wappinger's Falls, NY who, when she found herself late coming home from a meeting with a friend, invented a story to calm the anger of her step-father. Brawley, smeared herself with excrement, wrote the "N" word on her body and told those who found her wrapped in black plastic that she had been raped by members of the city police and one local attorney. Sharpton went on TV and accused the alleged rapists of racial wrong doing. Later, under questioning of police and social workers, Brawley admitted the ruse, but the damage had been done. The attorney, Steven Pagones, was sued for divorce by his wife. Pagones sued Sharpton for eighty-five thousand dollars and won.

Not one cent was ever paid by Sharpton. All this occurred in 1987-88. Years later, Sharpton would be awarded a job as a commentator for MSNBC. It has been alleged that Sharpton has visited the Obama White House over one hundred times. Mr. President, you have become a racist, and there is more to the story of this American President who seems to want to disrespect his country. Let's see what your friend, Sharpton, did in Ferguson.

Sharpton marched arm-in-arm with Michael Brown's family. He called for social justice and for the police department in Ferguson to fire the officer who shot Brown. The police officer was set upon by angry protesters and accused of shooting the "Gentle giant", Michael Brown. Two days later, protesters staged a candlelight vigil for Brown. The vigil turned into violent vandalizing and looting. Shortly afterward, "Black Lives Matter" raised its ugly head and T-shirts and hoodies emblazoned with that slogan were worn by protesters and looters. When one politician suggested that "All lives matter", he was shouted down and criticized as being intolerant.

It is very difficult to feel any sympathy for those who use the death of a young person to justify violence and looting. But when an American President sends his Attorney General, Eric Holder, to a town in turmoil, all the while knowing that his Attorney General will further fan the flames of discontent, that president is guilty of prejudice. There is still more reason to doubt the man presently in the White House.

On September 11, 2012, the American Embassy in Benghazi, Libya came under attack by anti-American Muslims. The American Ambassador, J. Christopher Stevens, was killed and dragged through the streets of Benghazi as U.S. government officials (both the Secretary of State, Hillary Clinton, and the President, Barack Obama), could not find a reason to call in reinforcements to aid Stevens' defenders. Three other Americans died from heavy smoke and fire set to the Embassy. Ten more were wounded which included non-military contractors who fought for thirteen hours holding off insurgents. The next day, U.S. officials (Susan Rice, an Under Secretary of State, and Hillary Clinton) told grieving families of those killed that the insurgency was caused by an American film directed by an American Muslim. The film, <u>The Innocence of Muslims</u>, and its notation by American officials seemed to justify the so-called spontaneous protest by Muslim insurgents. All this later dissipated when it was discovered that none of the insurgents knew anything about a movie. No one, including American media, pointed out that the attack occurred on September 11, the date of another Muslim massacre. To this date, no one, neither the former Secretary of State, Hillary Clinton, nor the President of the United States, Barack Obama, has been able to explain why no military assistance was sent to Benghazi to aid our American Ambassador and his men.

That question was carefully avoided in the film, <u>Thirteen Hours</u>, a film which portrayed the heroic attempts of former American service men to save the day. We, the United States, have the greatest military power in the world, yet not one fighter plane was sent to Libya on behalf of the besieged American defenders. Shame on you, Mr. President.

My disillusionment with my American President came from some of the above-mentioned shortcomings. Not all of the President's decisions have been discussed. The release of Bowe Bergdahl, the army deserter who, on a whim, decided that he needed to leave his unit and speak with the enemy, in exchange for captured Taliban fighters, all murderers, was and still is an enigma. The giving of automatic weapons to Mexican cartel members by Eric Holder, the former Attorney General under President Obama has never been clarified in spite of at least one Border Patrol officer being killed. The docking of all American Navy aircraft carriers just off the east coast of the United States in recent months for an extended period of time has indicated a less than effective decision making record, and that is undeniable. All that leads to the next scenario---the 2016 political campaign.

Politics and Race in 2016

At the moment of this writing, February 19, 2016, the American Presidential Campaign is in full swing. Republican and Democrat candidates for the presidency are parading across the stage in their efforts to rally support for their party and their platforms. All want to take the place of the man in the White House, Barack Obama. Let's take a look at the prospects.

My votes did not go for the first black-American President. In my lifetime, nothing comes to mind which would categorize me as racist. In high school on the football field and in the locker room, the ugly head of racial bias never seemed to come up. If you lived in Western Pennsylvania and played football, everyone on your team wore a helmet, and color played no part in how you felt about a fellow teammate. In the Marine Corps, we also wore helmets, and my fellow Marines, when injured, shed blood and whether you were black, white, or of any other color of skin, one's blood was always red. However, some enterprising journalist or attorney could convince a witness that, in the past, the "N" word was one of the words I uttered. Mark Furman would attest to that.

When the first-term Senator from Illinois won his first four years as President of the United States, my hopes were that he, our first black-American President would prove to be a uniting force in our country. That hope was soon dashed on the rocks of what seemed like the rubble of prejudice voiced by not only Barack Obama but also his wife.

Understandingly, black Americans support President Obama in almost every decision-making move he decides. After all, he is the first black-American President in our nation's history. But, in the opinion of many Americans, Barack Obama has become the most divisive president ever to reside in the White House. When it was first brought to light that Obama had been a member of a black-activist church, the Trinity United Church in Chicago, people began to question his religious leanings. On the surface, the liberal media saluted Obama's stand. But, more was to come to light about where the President stood on race relations.

It is very difficult to feel any sympathy for those who use the death of a human being to justify violence and looting in any society. However, if the American President fans the flames of social unrest, continually criticizes those who serve the public in security positions, and overlooks the results of his actions, there is little one can do. But, Americans do vote, and they are indicating that they are tired of political correctness and what seems to be racial bias.

The 2016 Political Primaries

In early February, the New Hampshire Primary took place. Presidential hopefuls in both the Democrat and Republican parties closed ranks and then settled in on the State of Iowa. Voters decided that Hillary Clinton and Bernie Sanders were tied in the number of Democrat votes cast, something the Clinton camp had not foreseen. In what is only understood by Iowa voters, a strange way of deciding who actually won took place. Clinton seemed to come out ahead of Sanders in that race. On the Republican side, Ted Cruz, Donald Trump and Marco Rubio were the top three contenders. New Hampshire showed the opposite for the Republicans; Trump, Cruz and Rubio came out on top in that order, and as time goes on, there seems to be more and more fingers pointed at the Obama administration and its questionable policies which is causing so many candidates to run for office.

The devastation in the form of racial upheaval, high unemployment levels, a confusing health plan, lack of support for the military and other nefarious decisions made by an ineffective Congress have brought out those who have never voted before. Americans are tired of full-time politicians who line their pockets by getting early information on stock options and who, for six months of the year, run for another term in office. So, here they come, presidential candidates who want to represent the strongest freedom-loving nation in history.

On the Democrat side of the docket, Hillary Clinton, the former Senator from the State of New York who never lived in that state until she decided to run for Congress. Former Secretary of State under President Obama, Clinton was head of the state department when the Benghazi fiasco occurred. Now, after weeks of political speeches, Clinton is the expected winner who will represent her party in the presidential election later this year. Bernie Sanders, the Jewish-American socialist, is a close second, and his supporters, mostly young Americans who want to see entitlements expanded, are helping the seventy-plus year old candidate. Michael Bloomberg, a multimillionaire businessman and former mayor of New York City, might be a late, unannounced candidate for the Democrats. That Bloomberg would carry the State of New York is understood; Democrats have controlled that state for years. Let's take a closer look at Sanders.

According to his speeches, Sanders wants free college education for all Americans, an increased minimum wage, increased entitlement spending and higher taxes for the superrich. While attractive to many Americans, this increased government spending would mean higher taxes for all, and the national debt is already at nineteen trillion dollars, an amount which is dragging the country toward the brink of collapse. The other Democrat, Hillary Clinton, is swiftly coming under scrutiny for her raking in millions of dollars for book publications and political speeches. She is also under surveillance for her use of unsecure e-mail servers while Secretary of State. No one, not the media nor Congress seems interested in searching reasons for her lack of action during the Benghazi fiasco. I must now wonder how so many Americans see strength in any of the above candidates. Are the Republicans any better?

In America today, a number of teenagers are caught up in SIW, self-inflicted wounds. Razor blades, knives, pins and clamps are used to inflict open wounds. Psychologists don't seem to know exactly why someone would want to harm himself, but evidence does point to those who cannot seem to get attention any other way. The 2016 Republican candidates mirror such foolishness. In most of the Republican debates from January through the end of February, candidates line up on stage and verbally deface their opponents' platforms. Name calling, insinuations about families, professions, marriages, and education take place. Dirty-trick TV ads concerning polling numbers and other less than socially accepted forays have eviscerated each Republican candidate more than if a coroner's knife had opened the most vital parts of a candidate's body. These incisions made on the same-party candidate's platforms have produced a bloodletting which must make the Democrats applaud. Senseless!

Donald Trump, the multimillionaire businessman and non- politician, has been the frontrunner of the Republican candidates.

While not yet receiving the blessing of the RNC, Trump has been the favorite of the disenfranchised American public. Voters are more and more critical of a Congress which seems uninterested in solving problems such as entitlements, illegal aliens crossing U.S. borders and the growing national debt. Congress is seen as an elite group of effete old men and women. The competency of members of Congress is questioned when some of this august body question whether an island in the Pacific will topple over if too many Marines are stationed on its shores. Congress is seen as a group of people too interested in keeping themselves in office. Some Americans are looking for a man or woman whose primary profession is not politics. So far, that person is Donald Trump.

In my research on Trump, my opinion of the candidate has remained cautious. Brought up in wealth, schooled in the New York State Military Academy, a school for adolescents who needed a disciplined curriculum, and for a short time, an athlete, Trump learned that hard work led to achievement. Later, in undergraduate school at Fordham, and again at the University of Pennsylvania's Wharton School of Business, Trump honed his skills at making money. By all accounts, he has done pretty well.

Donald Trump speaks his mind. He seems to be saying things a lot of Americans have been thinking but hesitate to state. Trump uses language seldom heard from other so-called respectable politicians. He is often portrayed in the political cartoons of liberal newspapers (The Arizona Republic) as a foul-mouthed monster who holds nothing back in his verbal depictions of opponents. Many Americans are fed up with the concept of political correctness spouted by a liberal press and other media talking heads. But, will this non-politician survive the attacks made on him by fellow Republicans and the RNC? That remains to be seen. Perhaps the American public will make that decision in the weeks ahead. But, other Republican candidates for the presidency are dropping by the wayside. Chris Christie, the Governor of New Jersey dropped out of the race last week and almost immediately threw his support to Donald Trump. Ted Cruz, a Senator from Texas; Marco Rubio, a

Senator from Florida; John Kasich, the Governor of Ohio; and Ben Carson, a retired neurosurgeon, are still in the running for the Republican candidacy for president. Carson is the only other non-politico other than Trump in the race for the Republican side. Carson shows a good knowledge of American history. As a black American who pulled himself up from poverty, he has a good sense of what a work ethic can do. In spite of that redeeming quality, Carson remains at the bottom of the choices offered Republican voters.

Kasich, Cruz and Rubio are the remaining potential candidates in the Republican camp. Kasich touts his success as being the governor who brought the State of Ohio into economic stability. Cruz sees his strength as having bucked the RNC and its establishment in Washington. Rubio has the electricity of youth, and his parents emigrated to the U.S. from Cuba. That could help win the Hispanic vote.

It is still too early (29 February) to make predictions here. My knowledge of politics is not such that my opinions would be of merit.

But, I do know that Americans are angry. Their anger is directed toward a do-nothing Congress and toward a President who has been less than effective in eliminating race as a source of frustration. The United States is faced with the threat of a rabid group of Islamic zealots. For some unknown reason, the U.S. Immigration Service and the Department of State are granting Muslims access to this country from places around the world which are strictly anti-American. And, many Americans are not ready to put goat on the table for Thanksgiving.

But, the <u>Quran</u> encourages the readers of this book to propagate and prosper in all the lands on this Earth. The United States is seen as fertile ground because of its liberal laws and tolerance. We are now faced with what has been termed as "home-grown terrorists," the children of Muslim parents living in the United States who see themselves as messengers of the faith. It is not my intention to cite all the insane killings performed on our soil by crazed Islamic followers.

The mere mention of Boston, San Bernardino and Fort Hood is enough to cause Americans to wonder why they have opened the doors to so many Muslims. But there are other reasons why Americans are looking forward to the November 2016 election.

Entitlements, often referred to as giving handouts to able-bodied individuals who should be working an eight to five job, is a source of frustration to those who get up every morning and commute to work.

The welfare system, a supplement which keeps individuals from ever looking for valid employment, has created families whose members have never had a job. Such a system has taken away pride in oneself, and that is an extension of slavery; a person made dependent upon something handed out by others is never really free. The astronomically high salaries of CEO's in our nation's economy is also a source of frustration to those who are working for a little pay.

Outsourcing, manufacturing jobs sent to Mexico, China and other countries throughout the world, has disenfranchised a large portion of the American public. Americans are tired of politicians. Enter Donald Trump.

At the time of this writing, the Iowa, New Hampshire and South Carolina primaries are over. For the Democrats, Hillary Clinton seems to be the clear favorite with Bernie Sanders still in the race, but a distant second. For the Republicans, Trump is still out in front of Rubio who has been using every crude innuendo to further his cause.

He accuses Trump of being a "con man", clown, and one who uses too much spray tan. But, in doing so, Rubio is beginning to sound like a sandlot junior high school bully. In essence, instead of addressing issues dear to the American public, Republican candidates are continuing to wound themselves with verbal barbs thrown daily in the media. Americans are still wondering what kind of President Trump would make. Most of us know that instead of building his own platform, Trump would hire people more competent than himself Trump's choices for his cabinet would probably have paid their taxes. One can only wait and see.

Update: March 3, 2016. This morning, Mitt Romney, a former Republican presidential candidate against Barack Obama in 2012, gave a speech at the University of Utah. He accused Donald Trump of being a phony, a person who is not a huge financial success, a person who, if he won the nomination for president, would lead our nation to ruin. Romney, a loser in his last attempt at running for office, a person who was afraid to confront Obama about Benghazi, is criticizing the current front runner of being incompetent. The RNC is apparently backing Romney in this venture, and it harkens back to what has already been said about the Republican establishment; self-inflicted wounds will bring down both candidates and party. How tired many Americans are of seeing politicos destroy each other. But, such a move will strengthen American resolve to elect someone other than a politician. Maybe, just maybe, we are making progress.

Racism Redux and the Oscars

A few nights ago, February 28, Hollywood delivered its annual "Look at me and tell me how great I am."- Oscar Night. No black American actor was nominated for an Oscar in 2016. It wasn't long before the race baiters threw their card on the stage. Spike Lee, always one of the first to complain about what he sees as inequality, declared the evening to be "White Oscar night." He immediately declared that he would not attend the ceremony. Al Sharpton, MSNBC's lapdog, and one of the worst to fan the flames of racism, called for a blackout of the TV broadcast. Will Smith's wife instantly declared that she would not attend the event, in spite of the fact that she was not invited. But, something was overlooked before all this clamoring took place; no one mentioned past black American winners of the coveted award.

In 2013, Chiwetel Ejiofor and Lupita Nyogio, both black actors, won Oscars for "12 Years a Slave". Other recent black-American winners of the award were Halle Berry, Cuba Gooding and Morgan Freeman. Not mentioning that fact is suspicious in nature. It should be pointed out that Barack Obama, in his almost deliberate attempt to encourage black outrage might have contributed to the backlash against the Oscars. And, the black-American comic actor, Chris Rock acted as Master of Ceremonies for this year's awards, and he made no attempt to hide his rancor.

Rock presented several clips of himself as portraying white Americans in their films. In a space suit, Rock imitated Matt Damon's portrayal of "The Martian". Dressed in animal skins, Rock panned DiCaprio's rendition of an early 19th century fur trapper. It was alluded to the audience that black actors could have played the same roles...perhaps better.

Political correctness once again raised its ever-becoming hideous head. But, something good did take place during the presentation of this year's Oscars; I cannot remember hearing one utterance and use of the "N" word, and this is all the more surprising since the Master of Ceremonies was a black American, i.e., and ironically, most often, the use of such a vulgar term is done by black Americans. For me, the use of such trash words, off limits to all but black Americans, is boring. The overuse of the "N" word by black Americans is degrading to the very people it is used to describe. But, if we are to rid our vocabularies of this despicable reference, we must also point out that the use of "honkey" and "cracker" must also be scrapped by all Americans. But, let's take one last look at Spike Lee's "white Oscar night".

Lee is supposedly a world-class film maker. If that is true, why hasn't this man made an effort to produce and direct films that showcase black-American actors? Certainly, such a feat requires work, and if Lee would spend more time in the creative use of his talents instead of spreading the race argument, he might even provide the viewing public with something worth watching. Lee, Woopie Goldberg, Al Sharpton and yes, the President of the United States, should call attention to black-Oscar winners who have graced the stage in the past. But, as long as the Master of Ceremonies, Chris Rock, ends this year's Oscar night with the quip, "Black lives matter", we are still a long way from erasing black and white hatred in this country.

Cell Phones and Selfies

Ubiquitous in essence, seemingly indispensable to almost everyone, the clamor for instant gratification and attention seems to have led to an inexhaustible supply of machines used for communication and attention getting. Let's look at the American addiction to cell phones and their use.

One evening not too long ago, my wife and I decided to take dinner at a local trendy restaurant in Scottsdale, Arizona. Eating out is not something we often do; happy hours with friends is more fun and less dangerous than after a cocktail or two at a restaurant. Once we were seated, had looked over the menu and ordered our meal, other diners began to arrive and fill in the seating area. Two young people drew our attention.

An attractive thirty something man and woman took a table across from ours. The first thing the young couple did, even before looking over a menu, was to put out in front of them, both the man and his companion, the omnipresent cell phone. Even before ordering their meal, each one stationed their phones in front of them, turned them on and began texting and scrolling. Without ever looking at their wait person who began taking their order, the young couple seemed to idolize that lit-up screen in front of them. As if they were in a trance, their eyes were fixed on the thing in front of them. For the next hour, at least while my wife and I finished our dinner, not a word was uttered between the young man and his companion. My words to my wife were, "Isn't it nice having dinner with each other." Cell phones can freeze human tongues. But, there is more evidence that people are mesmerized by their phones.

Put yourself in an airline terminal. You are waiting for your plane, and you decide to relax and watch the crowd of travelers go by. All sizes, shapes, colors, all forms of dress and people of all ages parade as if marching in some homecoming event at a university. A cornucopia spills out the peoples of all nations who, at first glance, seem different. But, they have at least one thing in common; they have cell phones, and most of these machines are in use.

If you sit and watch closely, most of your fellow travelers are fully engaged with their favorite toy. Conversations are taking place with invisible companions, texting is taking place and sent over the wireless network, scrolling is providing information at a rapid rate to hundreds of super-focused individuals. The eyes of these totally involved travelers are lowered as if giving respect to some god or deity. It makes one wonder whether anyone would notice if a sudden calamity took place. Perhaps not; people do love their phones.

Have you ever gone grocery shopping and found yourself wondering if someone was addressing you? In the past, people talking to themselves would have drawn stares, and we might have looked away thinking, "That poor crazy thing!" I sometimes find myself responding to a person who is in an aisle close to me looking right at me saying, "Do I need tomatoes?" I say, "Oh, I wouldn't know." Then the tomato person says, "Oh, no, I was on my Bluetooth." Doesn't anyone make a grocery list anymore? But, let's get serious. Cell phones do come in handy.

Over a year ago, I was on my way for an early-morning pickle ball game. During rush hour around 7:30 A.M., I was traveling on a three-lane highway and obeying the 45 mph limit. All three lanes of the right of way in my direction were filled, and my car was in the middle lane. Cars in front of me, on both sides of me and behind me were observing the speed limit...all except one. In my rear-view mirror, I could see a car coming at what looked to be eighty miles an hour. There was nothing for me to do but wait for the impact, and sure enough, it came. The car behind me hit my auto with such force that the rear of my car collapsed, and I was projected forward and forced to take evasive action. Without being propelled forward into the car in front of me, I somehow managed to get to the side of the road without hitting cars alongside of me. Once stopped, the car which hit me from behind, pulled in front of me to the side of the road and stopped. Almost immediately, a young woman got out of the car holding something in her hand. Yep, a cell phone, and she was still in a conversation with someone on the other end.

The young woman rushed up to my car and shouted, "Are you OK? I'll give you my insurance cards, but I am late for work and have to go on." Now, I was not seriously injured. But, I had to say to this unfortunate person the following: "Young lady, if you even attempt to leave the area, your license plate number will be given to the first policeman who arrives, and you will be cited as having left the scene of an accident." That seemed to calm down the cell-phone caller. The young woman was given a citation a few minutes later. My auto was repaired, my hospital bills paid, and my insurance deductible was returned to me. A settlement for the accident has never been paid, but that is another story. What I did not have with me in my car the day of the accident was...a cell phone. I think I have one now, but I don't know where it is. Let's be frank; having a phone in your car is a good idea. That it should only be used when the car is in park is a better idea. And, here is another.

How many times have we seen a TV broadcast showing some bystander's cell phone video of an accident, crime or catastrophe? It is becoming a common occurrence to view the cell-phone filming of such things. There is no longer a dire need for cameras on every corner of a bustling city; hundreds of them are moving along the walkways in the hands of curious human beings. Our innocent acts on the street are open season for roving unofficial journalists. That's probably a good thing. Numerous officers of the law have been given scrutiny by pedestrians coming across an altercation. And, that prevalence of having a phone in hand has given rise to something else---selfies.

There is probably no place like Face Book to observe our narcissistic propensity to take our own photo. Our cell phones seem to await the next photo like lions in a zoo waiting for the next feeding. Face Book provides us with the evidence that taking our own photo is worth the effort. We get instantaneous return from friends saying, "Wow! That must have been a great trip. How much fun you must have had." In taking that selfie, one seems to say, "Look at me. See where I am? This is me." Where did all this self-gratification come from? There might be a simple answer. In a society where "Dancing with the Stars" is one of our most popular TV shows, and where Hollywood parades its workers across the stage on Oscar Night, we, too, seek our fifteen minutes of fame. Grocery store tabloids splash the latest love story, scandal, or impending death of a celebrity in front of our eyes. The thought comes up, "Me, too." And our cell phones are ever ready to satisfy our thirst for showing how we fit into this world. And, something has just been invented which makes it easier to include us in the mix---selfie sticks. With a yard-long pole and our camera/ cell phone attached at the end, we can include a host of friends or dignitaries in our museum of events where we played a role. Is that bad? Come on! Really, this is part of where we are today. Get used to it. Say, "Cheese!".

Religions

Thanks to my maternal grandmother, a wonderful, devoted, loving, hard-working woman, I was introduced to church. While she rarely had time for such things (she earned her living by taking in washing and ironings from well-to-do townspeople), my grandmother seemed to realize that being introduced to religion might somehow benefit me. She took time from her busy schedule to escort me to the First Methodist Church in our little Susquehanna River town. When I was six years old, my attendance at Sunday school lasted only three or four times; a hard-working woman doesn't have the luxury to escort her grandson to many places, and my grandmother never had enough money to purchase an automobile.

Grandmother must have been a Methodist. At least, that's where she took me on those few occasions.

Those few visits to her church were the last times I went to church until my enlistment at the age of seventeen in the United States Marine Corps. When asked by my Parris Island D.I. what religion I professed, my immediate response was, "Sir, Methodist, Sir". From that day on, my dog tags read, "Methodist". So, I must be a Methodist. No one disputes a Marine Corps D.I.'s designation.

In boot camp, on Sunday mornings, recruits were separated into Protestant and Catholic groups and marched off to outdoor services. That was in 1957. Today, if religious activities are still allowed, more religious denominations are probably placed accordingly. But, those Sunday morning worship sessions gave young men and women a reprieve from the scrutiny of the all-knowing, all-seeing D.I.'s, and every night after lights out, I silently recited the 23rd psalm and asked God to make me the best Marine possible. My feeling is this: without the opportunity to express my needs to a being superior to me, the thirteen weeks at Parris Island would have been more difficult.

Two years later, near the end of my enlistment, my fiancée joined me in Hawaii. We were married in the 1st Methodist Church in Honolulu. Three other people attended the ceremony---the minister, the church matron and the custodian. God might have been there, too.

Unfortunately, I do not attend regular church services. No formal baptism has ever taken place for me. But, my belief in an immortal power greater than man is as strong as ever. My belief that Jesus Christ was perhaps the world's greatest perfect individual is unwavering, and my daily, silent prayers are directed to him and his father. But, I never preach my own beliefs other than setting them to type in such a form as this. My intellect is not strong enough to see through all the mysteries which are offered up for interpretation. Everyone in his own way should try to figure out the meaning of life. And, there's the rub. Too many of the world's people become zealots, and Hell is let loose on humanity.

From my reading and experience, human beings have been trying to figure out the answers to Paul Gauguin's three basic questions: (Who are we? Where are we? Where are we going?). Humans have been trying to answer those questions for thousands of years. In caves where our ancestors lived over twenty thousand years ago, hand prints and paintings have been discovered. Those depictions of life seem to say, "This is me." Prehistoric selfies stating that human lives matter are found in such caves. Ancient people worshiped the sun, the moon and the trees, and they would kill others who disputed their choice of a deity.

Long before Islam came to light in the sixth century in the Middle East, battles were fought because others had a god different from that accepted by their neighbors. In 732 A.D., Charles Martel stopped the fanatic surge of Islam in the middle of France. After that,

Christians began their crusades to the Holy Land trying to preserve religious sites. Zealots come in all forms, and millions have paid the price because of intolerance. Expecting such bigotry to end in our lifetime is a consummation devoutly to be wished.

Most everyone is aware of the turmoil which took place and is still smoldering in Northern Ireland. Protestants against Catholics is an issue which seems to have no end. Their God is the same, a crucifix is hung in both the denominations' churches, but no one can see the others' good qualities. It does not seem to be a matter of blood or color. Each side expects the other to worship in only one way. Sunni Muslims hate Shia Muslims. Both sides are from the same family history which took place years ago. No matter. "My ancestor was more legitimate than yours." "My way is better." How petty! How ridiculous! But, there is a term for all this tension.

In the 1960's, Eric Hoffer, a California dock worker, wrote a book entitled,

<u>The True Believer</u>. In his writing, Hoffer outlines the thoughts of those who see only their way of thinking. He pointed out that Adolph Hitler saw a certain sect as evil. He envisioned a race of people whose physical characteristics were superior to all others. He believed those things unhesitatingly. He was a true believer. That belief was so strong that it led to the death of millions of innocent people. The total adherence to a dogma at the exclusion of all other ideas can and does lead to abuse. Islam has intercepted the evil expressed in Germany in the 30's and 40's, and it is running wild.

The Middle East and other parts of the world are in turmoil because of a fanatical belief in Islam. Those true believers are the same ones who do not want fifty percent of their population (women) to go to school. In some Islamic countries, only boys go to school and they are forced into a head-bobbing memorization of the <u>Quran</u> until they are fully indoctrinated and found "worthy" of pursuing higher education. Unfortunately, this higher education sometimes has to do with constructing IED's used to maim and kill those who did not bend toward the accepted dogma taught in the region. And, God forbid if someone professed another religion such as Judaism or Christianity.

No Christian church or Jewish synagogue may be built in Saudi Arabia. In certain Islamic countries, the wearing of a crucifix or the Star of David can lead to death for the wearer. In the United States, an Islamic mosque is built every month. Are Americans too tolerant? Perhaps. But, we do not tear down the religious icons of those whose beliefs are different from our own. We do not desecrate the cemeteries and grave stones of those who think differently from us as is now the case in Libya and other North African nations. How do we encourage tolerance in the world? Once again, my intellect is not great enough to suggest a panacea for such thing. But, I do know that my God would not tolerate my taking the life of another unless I was back in combat fighting for survival or to quell some terrible uprising.

As stated above, my dog tags read Methodist. My two children are Catholic. I love them both. Always will. And, as for those who profess no religion, whether they are agnostic or atheist, let them live in peace and not be worried about others who are in need of direction and spiritual sustenance. Will those who profess no religion be as tolerant as possible? Time will tell.

Blood Relations and Cousins

Is there anything better than family? Blood relations, the gene pool, DNA, accents, and family traits---great stuff. But, those relationships you establish in little groups like happy hours, they, too, become family after a while. Blood does not have to be part of that mix. Togetherness is a comfortable thing. When you find yourself with a group of people who share their stories with you, and yours with them, that's a good thing. It indicates trust, a thin bond and common ground. And, no one gets killed in such groups.

My aunts and uncles were people I admired. All of them seemed to have a certain *Je ne sais quoi,* a certain strength of character which made them special to me. When my grandmother's children would come to visit their mother, I would marvel at the love and appreciation expressed at those get togethers. At the time, I wondered why I was included in those meetings; I was young, not from a part of the family that had economic security, and no one thought I was going anywhere fast. It was in these groups where I met my cousins, a great circle of young people.

None of my cousins ever treated me with disrespect. It didn't seem to matter that I lived in a little two-room shack with no central heating, no water and two electric lights. These blood relations were kind. Now, all my aunts and uncles have passed. Some of my cousins have followed them, all too quickly. Of those who remain on this Earth, they are all important to me. Let me name those who remain: Shirley, Earl, Sandy, Cheryl, Phyllis and Sue. I can still beat Earl in Indian wrestling. I can't beat Shirley, Sandy, Cheryl, Phillis or Sue, but I can beat Earl. How important is blood in our relationships. Let's take a look at it in the next chapter.

Blood, Sweat and Human Evolution

In light of all the religious intolerance and rabid racism which prevails around the world, attention should be called to a study encouraged by the National Geographic Society. In 2005, while reading one of the issues of NGS, my interest was drawn to a study conducted by Dr. Miquel Vilar, a molecular anthropologist. Dr. Vilar and others with like academic training were calling upon readers of the magazine to take part in a study which traced one's DNA back over thousands of years. To become a participant in this study, readers were asked to send a small fee in return for a swab kit meant to collect one's DNA. My wife and I both sent for the kit, and when it arrived, we followed procedures and returned our swab samples to the appropriate laboratory. Ten weeks later, we received the results of our samples.

We did not know that Dr. Vilar's study had been in progress for ten or more years prior to our submission of our DNA. The results of this study are worth mentioning.

Over a period of fifteen years, molecular scientists traversed the Earth's surface collecting DNA samples from thousands of human beings. Results showed that humans had left the African continent about a hundred thousand years ago and began populating other parts of the world. All the groups took the same route out of Africa. Across Egypt and up the Sinai Peninsula through what is now Syria, small groups of these early migrants then fanned off to the west and into central Western Europe. Other groups turned east and north to Siberia and then south into India. Along the way and over thousands of years, interesting physical characteristics evolved with our ancestors.

It does appear that the first humans to leave Africa a hundred thousand years ago were dark skinned. There is good reason for that. The intensity of the sun's rays could cause havoc with exposed skin. If our ancestors lived in Africa a hundred thousand years ago, nature provided for them by putting into play the evolution of the human skin. It became darker and protected those who wore only scant clothing. But, when migrants started to work their way north and out of the African continent, skin color changed again. For those who headed for colder climates, something was needed to allow the sun's energy to penetrate the body. Humans began to wear animal skins to protect themselves from more severe climates. Nature again played a role in human evolution. Skin became lighter which allowed easy access to for vitamin D to enter through lighter skin. Thus, chemicals needed for survival shows evidence of the body's ability to adapt. That might prove true later when space exploration requires longer periods of time in weightlessness for astronauts. The important thing is this: we all came out of Africa, and at one time in our history, all our ancestors were black. And, all of our blood was of different types, but it was all red.

In the case of my wife and I, we learned some important information. My wife's ancestors left Africa about 85,000 years ago. My ancestors came out of that same continent 10,000 years later. So, now I realize why my wife has always been ahead of me. But, there are other changes which took place in the human body over those thousands of years of migration.

Those individuals who turned east and west as they crossed Egypt and Syria and into Siberia faced harsh conditions. Snow, ice, chilling winds and low temperatures made the human body respond and produce changes over thousands of years. If you live above the Mason-Dixon Line in the United States, you have probably encountered winter snow storms. That blowing snow and sleet makes one squint in order to tolerate the harsh conditions as you walk from place to place. In Siberia, those who crossed that expansive area and went on to Japan and the United States by crossing the land bridge connecting Asia and Alaska, developed a change in facial development; eyes began to slant in order to provide better sight during inclement conditions.

Human growth and development over the last two thousand years has implications. If we all came out of Africa as scientific study suggests, if our ancestors' skin was dark or black, and if we have similar strains of blood, we are related to one another. What is all the insane adherence to race, religion and color? We all came out of Africa, damn it. Get over yourselves.

Roe vs Wade and Infanticide

If there is any Supreme Court case which has led to a difference of opinion in the United States, it is perhaps the decision made by that court in 1973 entitled Roe v. Wade. There is hardly a moment in TV presidential debates between candidates for the presidency where the above case is not discussed. On the decision of the Supreme Court, a 7-2 ruling declared that a right to privacy under the Due Process Clause of the Fourteenth Amendment allows a woman to have an abortion. But, this right must be balanced against the state's two legitimate interests in regulation abortions protecting women's health and protecting the potentiality of human life. Let's look at the dictionary definition of abortion.

Merriam-Webster's says that abortion is, "the termination of a pregnancy after, accompanied by, resulting in, or closely followed by the death of the embryo or fetus; the spontaneous expulsion of a human fetus during the first 12 weeks of gestation; the expulsion of a fetus by a domestic animal often due to infection; and the induced expulsion of a human fetus." To me, abortion is equivalent to the taking of a life. Whether the taking of a life is justifiable is something we should consider, and there are at least two camps of followers in this matter.

If you are among those who support abortion, you are said to be pro-choice. Those who are against abortion are said to be pro-life. Sometimes, if you are in the pro-life group, you are accused of declaring a war on women. I wonder if anyone seems to want to consider the life of the unborn fetus. One of the most profound statements on this issue came from a friend of mine from Canada. He said, "Those who are for abortion are those who were already allowed to be born." It is almost as if those already born do not want to share in the beauties of life experiences.

Life is such a precious thing. To deny the joys, tribulations and challenges that life offers is a modern-world tragedy. However, there are reasons why abortion should be allowed and made legal. If a woman has been raped, if she has been the victim of incest, if the mother's health is in jeopardy or if the fetus is in danger of being born with a serious deformity or defect, then, by all means, abortion should take place. And, then, too, the woman should have the right to decide. But, there is another matter. Does a man have a role to play in this decision? Do men's lives matter?

Without question, a woman's body is first and foremost the important aspect up for consideration. But, shouldn't the father, if legitimately an entity in the equation, be given some say whether his son or daughter should be given life? For all too long, the male has taken a back seat in this female-driven bus. But, let's take another look at "Roe" in Roe v. Wade.

In 1969, Norma L. McCorvey became aware that she was pregnant with her third child. Living in Texas, she went to Dallas where her friends advised her to claim that she had been raped, and therefore, under Texas law, would be able to obtain a legal abortion. However, since no police record showed any evidence of McCorvey's claim, the mother was denied her right to abortion. Norma L. McCorvey gave birth before the Supreme Court ruled in her favor.

In 1970, Linda Coffee and Sarah Weddington filed suit in McCorvey's behalf in the United States District Court under the alias of Jane Roe. Instead of the male counterpart, John Doe, McCorvey became Jane Roe. The Texas court ruled against Roe in the case. But, in the same year, the case went before the Supreme Court. In 1973, with a 7-to-2 majority vote in favor of Roe, the Court deemed abortion a fundamental right under the United States Constitution. In doing so, the majority opinion explicitly rejected a fetal "right to life" argument.

Since 1973, millions of abortions have taken place. Millions of lives have been snuffed out. But, once again, let's return to Linda McCorvey a.k.a. Jane Roe.

Ironically, in 1995, Norma L. McCorvey announced to the public that she had become pro-life, and she joined those who opposed abortion. In 1998, she testified to Congress: "It was my pseudonym, Jane Roe, which had been used to create the "right" to abortion out of legal thin air. But, Sarah Weddington and Linda Coffee (Roe's attorneys in 1970) never told me that what I was signing would allow women to come up to me 15, 20 years later and say, 'Thank you for allowing me to have my first five or six abortions. Without you, it wouldn't have been possible.' Sarah never mentioned women using abortions as a form of birth control. We talked about truly desperate and needy women, not women already wearing maternity clothes."

The Constitution plays a part in granting abortion. Under the Thirteenth Amendment, women who are compelled to carry and bear children are subject to involuntary servitude. Under the Fourteenth Amendment, the right to privacy under the Due Process Clause allows women to make a choice as to whether they carry their pregnancy to term. Thus, women do have the right to terminate the life of their fetus. Men who contributed to life's process have no such rights in this decision. And, the fact remains that millions of living fetus will never see the light of day. Those minute creatures will never experience the joys, sorrows, pleasures and experiences that those who read these words have encountered. <u>C'est la vie? Non! C'est la mort.</u>

Nellie Bly, Columbine and Deinstitutionalization

After the news media issues a report of another mass murder or shooting incident, what are some of the first things which come to mind? Do you say to yourselves, "What in the world is going on?" "How could this happen?" "Who would do such a thing?" Once the evil of the crime is internalized, we read newspaper accounts, and we watch TV interviews which try to analyze the perpetrators of these heinous acts. Neighbors and family members of the person who committed the crime will sometimes say, "Oh, he (she) was such a kind and considerate individual." "He (she) never gave any indication of being disturbed." Bah, humbug! If we look at what has taken place in the United States over the last century, we might be able to better understand why such bad things happen. And, a young woman from Pittsburgh might have contributed to the problem.

Elizabeth Cochran Seaman was born in the Pittsburgh, PA area in 1864. At boarding school, she became offended with a misogynistic article, "What Girls Are Good For", which appeared in the Pittsburgh Dispatch. Elizabeth wrote a rebuttal to the editor of that newspaper under the pseudonym, "Lonely Orphan Girl". The editor was so impressed with Elizabeth's article that he offered her a full-time job as a journalist. In those days, women newspaper writers customarily used pennames. Enamored with the music of another Pittsburgh resident, Stephen Foster, Elizabeth chose the name, "Nelly Bly" from one of Foster's songs. Her editor misspelled "Nelly" by mistake and wrote, "Nellie". The name stuck.

Later in her career, Nellie Bly became famous for her work at the New York World when, in 1888, she made an effort to see if it was possible to turn Jules Verne's Around the World in Eighty Days into fact. Bly completed the trip in less time that it took for Verne's character, Phileas Fogg, to do the same thing. But, for our purposes here, Bly did something else which has significance in the present day.

In 1887, Nellie Bly left Pittsburgh for New York City. Using her charm and persistence, she made her way into the <u>New York World</u> and the offices of Joseph Pulitzer. Pulitzer allowed his new journalist a chance to look into the goings on in a local mental institution. Bly feigned insanity by checking into a boarding house. Then, for the next two nights, she screamed, talked to imaginary people and drew the attention of two psychiatrists both of whom declared her to be insane. The next day, Bly was committed to Bellevue, a local asylum.

At Bellevue, Bly became a willing witness to the harsh conditions imposed on women patients. Gruel broth, spoiled meat and dirty undrinkable water was the diet for the inmates. The more dangerous patients were linked together by ropes. Human waste was observed around the eating places. Rats were everywhere competing for scraps left on the floors. Ice-cold water was poured over the heads of patients to keep them quiet. While she was there, Bly talked to several other women who, she thought, were as sane as she was. In one of her later newspaper articles, Bly wrote, "What, excepting torture, would produce insanity quicker than this treatment?"

Bly spent ten days at the asylum before Pulitzer had her released. Nellie published her report in book form under the title, <u>Ten Days in a Mad-House</u>, which, when read, encouraged an investigation into the conditions at the asylum. The results of that investigation caused a clamor as if someone had been bitten by a snake during church. For the next thirty years, mental institutions began closing their doors, and in doing so, the United States began to disperse mentally-disturbed individuals onto the streets.

In the beginning of the 20th century, subtle changes began to take place in and around mental institutions. Serious overcrowding, cuts in funding caused by economic downturns and wartime took place and more and more asylums became notorious for poor living conditions, lack of hygiene, ill-treatment and abuse of patients. A culminating activity of all this might have led to the 1948 movie, <u>The Snake Pit</u> in which Olivia de Havilland played a woman who went through treatment in a mental institution.

To ease the burden placed on asylums, the process of replacing long-stay psychiatric hospitals with less-isolated community mental health services for those with mental disorders began to emerge. That process was given the name, "deinstitutionalization". While some psychiatrists claim that deinstitutionalization has been an overall benefit for most psychiatric patients, many have been left homeless and without care. Instead of being monitored by well-trained practitioners, thousands of people with mental deficiencies are now walking our streets, driving automobiles, and buying guns. But, as time went on, things got worse.

Many states and, indeed, the federal government believed that legislation would create a nationwide network of locally-based mental health centers which, rather than large state hospitals, would be the main source of treatment for the mentally ill. But, a series of court decisions in the late 1960's that limited the commitment powers of state and local officials accelerated the discharge of mental patients. Many psychiatrists began prescribing Thorazine which is used for schizophrenia and depression. But, drugs only work as long as they are used according to prescription. Without daily supervision, either by a professional or a parent/guardian, things can go wrong. Many parents are reluctant to admit that their children are in need of mental health.

In 1955, in Ardmore, Oklahoma, a well-to-do oilman and his wife were waiting on the birth of their son. In Ardmore, a brand new hospital was to open the following day, but the prospective mother knew that a hospital nearer her home, Hardy Sanitarium, was going to close the following day, and she wanted to say that hers was the last baby born at that hospital. The baby was born and appeared to be completely normal. In the years to follow, it was discovered that the baby, now a young man, was psychotic. He would be kept at home and cared for by his affluent parents. The young man displayed a strange fascination for a young movie star, Jodie Foster. The man strayed from his medication. His name was John Warnock Hinckley, Jr.

In recent years, we have come to know and learn about such places as Fort Hood, the historic black church in Charleston, S.C., Columbine High School and the Umpqua Community College in Oregon. In fact, half of the deadliest shootings in United States history happened in the past six years. Our first inclination, and indeed, the first statement to come out of the mouths of the talking heads, is to blame the gun lobby. Mental illness does not seem to be a subject of discussion in the face of tragedy. Instead of advocating for more and better mental health care, we point our finger at the Second Amendment.

We avoid facts such as that which recently came to light in Maryland. Sixteen percent of those incarcerated in Maryland's prisons have been diagnosed with a mental illness. If we take into consideration those who kill for acts of passion, and if we question the cerebral capacity of those people, the percentage of mentally-disturbed people goes up. There is a national trend to push more patients out of mental hospitals and into community-based care, and some of those released have nowhere to go. Nellie Bly, what did you do?

Banjos, Harmonicas
and Four-Way Stops

In sixth grade, my small-town community was engaged in the building of a new school. The post-war baby boom produced an increase in school-age children, and new schools were de rigueur. To allow for construction to take place, some of us who lived near the center of town were bused every day to a neighboring hamlet which had declining enrollments and had available space for new students. What a treat. The first time on a school bus. Before that time, most of us who lived less than a mile and a half from school walked through all kinds of weather and in all degrees of temperature, "up hill, both ways." Such necessities made for a strong group of kids.

The new experience of attending a school six miles from home was exciting. Along the way, bus riders got the chance to see parts of the outlying districts they had never seen before. New sights, new friends, and new sounds of all sorts enveloped our lives. Television had not yet sapped the mind's ability to imagine, and the colors nature provided along the way to our new school was like watching a movie in Technicolor. And, a few of us learned something else; we found out that some of us were disadvantaged.

One day during recess, the hallmark of many grade-school goers, an auspicious on-looker arrived on the playground. The person, an important-looking woman, came into our outdoor area and asked that we return to our classrooms. We were told that we were going to be given a musical-aptitude test which would determine whether or not we could play a musical instrument. Those who passed the test were destined to play in the junior high school band. Those who did not pass the test, boys in particular, would go on to play football. After all, we lived in Pennsylvania.

Before any listening portions of the test were administered, we test takers had to answer a few questions. "What is your home like?" "Do you have a musical instrument at home?" "Where do your parents work?" "What does your father do?" At the time, I wondered what such things had to do with my ability to play an instrument. My mother had a Victrola and she would play Gene Krupa, Guy Lombardo, Glenn Miller and "Tales from the Vienna Woods" for me. What did such questions have to do with my recognizing a clarinet from a kettle drum? I did not pass the musical aptitude test. But, football was a lot of fun.

About the same time that my test givers told me that the music department would pass me by as a candidate for a career in music, I made an important discovery in my grandmother's attic. What a marvelous, mysterious place that attic was. Old clothes which dated into the last century laid about like discarded shrouds from lives gone by. Books written and published in the 19th century, button-up shoes, straw boater's hats, and a mishmash of cooking utensils no longer needed in the coal-stoked cooking stoves of modern times were strewn about like bodies from terrible Civil War battles. But, then, something caught my eye. An old, string-less banjo was propped up in a corner like some old friend waiting on me to find it in a game of hide-and-seek.

A little while later, banjo in hand and sitting in my grandmother's kitchen, coal stove going full blast, I eyed my wonderful grandmother and asked her if I could keep the beat-up old banjo. Grandmother never wavered when I would ask her for little things, and as long as it was within her power, she would grant me almost anything. I treasured that old thing. But, my instrument needed a tune up.

Without the first inkling of what a chord was, what strings were needed and how to go about putting strings on a banjo, my next steps took me to a small, local music store. There, the proprietor helped me along, sold me a cheap set of strings for my banjo and gave me a short lesson having to do with applying the strings to the instrument. A day of two later, my new banjo had a set of strings.

Finger picks in those days were not yet the accepted way to play the instrument, and my strumming caused my poor mother to develop a tremor. But, unfortunately, my strumming also drew the attention of one of our older neighbors. One day he asked me if he could borrow my machine. In those days, when an adult asked you for something, his wish was a command. The last time I saw that banjo was during a community talent show held at my school. The neighbor who had borrowed my instrument did a solo on stage. At the end of his song, I applauded. But, had it been in my hands I would have done better. I never saw my banjo again.

In the early 70's, a young comedian, playwright, actor, author and banjo player came to the town where I was teaching French at the local public high school. Our town had SPAC, the

Saratoga Performing Arts Center. My wife and I thought it a good idea to attend the concert/performance of the young comedian. Steve Martin was just starting his career, and in one of his skits, Martin played his banjo. Now, in the 21st century, Steve Martin is known as one of the world's best banjo players, and that performance played a role in increasing my interest in the five-string instrument. But, at the time, I was studying the harmonica.

One day, after a lesson at a local music store, I spotted an old banjo for sale in one of the music racks. I bought it, and started playing an instrument which had escaped me for so many years. My age, 70 at the time, didn't keep me from picking up where I had left off at the age of 12. Banjo lessons took the place of learning how to play the harmonica, and a musician's performance at SPAC had worked magic on me.

Not too long ago, the Philadelphia Philharmonic Orchestra came to town (Saratoga Springs) to spend its summer at SPAC, and, for the first time in my memory, a famous banjo player was to accompany the orchestra in a one-piece performance. Bela Fleck, one of the most accomplished pickers in American music, was the artist. Before his performance with the orchestra, Fleck was scheduled to take questions from those interested. For a small fee, one could ask this famous banjo player anything which came to mind. My wife bought me what happened to be the last ticket to this Q & A session. Off I went.

Mustering up the courage to ask one of the world's greatest banjo players questions about the five-string instrument was difficult. But, at the time, my plunking the strings had been going on for a few years, and one rarely gets such an opportunity to speak with a professional player. So, somewhere in the session, my hand shot up like some rocket launching at Cape Canaveral, and the musician looked at me and said, "Yes. What's on your mind?"

More than a hundred concert goers were on hand in a room at the arts center. In a somewhat halting voice, I spoke up and said, "Mr. Fleck, what advice would you give to a 74 year old who, at the age of 70 had decided to try playing the banjo?" Fleck took a deep breath and answered, "Well, the first thing you should do is say goodbye to all your friends." A roar of laughter came from the others in the room. Then, the banjo player continued with his answer saying that practice, patience and persistence would help, and that I should enjoy the years to come with my instrument. Since that time, I have tried to follow Fleck's advice. Most of my friends are still with me.

My harmonica is pulled out of its case from time to time, and if I am lucky, a recognizable tune comes forth. My father-in-law would perhaps be proud of my playing. He would often try his hand at playing the harp, but he was not one to take lessons from anyone. But, it is my banjo which occupies most of my time when trying to come up with a rendition of a tune. With practice, my interpretations of "Cripple Creek", "Blackberry Blossom", and "Foggy Mountain Breakdown" are recognizable, but my efforts will never reach the level of the recently-deceased Earl Scruggs. Few people will ever surpass him and his playing. So, thanks to my not being able to pass a sixth-grade musical aptitude test, I never played in the band. But, I rediscovered the pleasure of having a banjo.

In the next few short paragraphs, let me try to equate my learning how to play a stringed instrument with the rule of law. Timing, that placement of notes on a recognizable plane so that what occurs is pleasing to the ear is equivalent to doing the right thing in life. There is a certain harmony in doing what's right.

As with the harmonica, blowing or sucking air through the right hole produces a recognizable sound. If enough correct moves take place along the harmonica's board, smiles come to the faces of those who listen. The same thing takes place when people do the right thing at intersections where there is a four-way stop.

In almost every city and small town, intersections are governed by either an electric lighting system or a four-way stop. American motorists are used to the green/yellow/red sequence alerting them to the right-of-way on the road. The big, red STOP sign does the same thing. But, there are certain psychological nuances which occur at a four-way stop which are separate from the overhead light.

At a traffic light, the driver's focus is placed on a colored bulb. On green, the driver steps on the accelerator and is propelled forward into the line of traffic. On yellow, the driver's speed is reduced. On red, most automobiles come to a complete stop. All of this takes place without a glance at fellow drivers. We are like moths focused on the next light which tells us what to do. At a four-way stop, humanity begins to play its role.

When we approach an intersection governed by four stop signs, one on each corner, we look for other drivers. Courtesy usually governs who moves first. Most of us yield the right-of-way to the driver who arrived before our coming to a stop. We nod our heads in a gesture of permission to proceed or we indicate tolerance by flashing our lights to our fellow drivers allowing them the right-of-way. Good manners and courtesy bring a smile to our faces. We feel good about our little recognition of others. Is that always the case? Certainly not. But, I wonder if things would go better in Iraq, Afghanistan and Syria if, instead of dropping bombs, we would plant four-way stops at every road crossing. Worth a try.

Pseudointellectuals, 1-800 Numbers and Outsourcing

Celebrity Magazine, **People** and other super-market tabloids keep us informed about the rich and famous in our society. We watch "Hollywood Housewives" and "Keeping up with the Kardashians" as if our lives depended on it. But, such sitcoms are so over the top with glitter and gushing that they are becoming boring. What makes these people in front of the camera think that we might be somehow intrigued by the goings on in their lives, their latest love conquest or their recent divorce? We are constantly showered with the pictures showing how the rich and famous live. Yet, we buy the magazines and we watch the shows as though addicted by some magic powder. If we look closely, we discover something else about those who are putting on the Ritz.

Cleavage and creativity do not necessarily go hand in hand. We are led to believe by those who cover the

Hollywood set that those lucky enough to hold a leading role in a film are somehow smarter, more able and more sophisticated that the average American. Beauty and brains? Maybe not.

Look at Oscar night. Those who star in the latest blockbuster are paraded across the red carpet wearing Armani tuxes and twenty-thousand dollar gowns. When asked to speak, they read from scripted notes and invariably end with some personal message about the state of the Earth, American culture or race relations. What makes these people think that most of us are interested in what they say? The answer? Simple; they have been made to believe that winning an award for a performance makes them politically, socially and intellectually superior to you and me. Bovine scatology!

In Hollywood as in the TV studios, actors are governed by their handlers---the directors. The director suggests a pose, a mood, a range of emotions, accents and physical mannerisms which pertain to the character portrayed by the actor. The actor is led like some child in the hand of a hovering mother into a series of trials which might lead to perfection. Practice, many retakes and different camera angles are conducted, photo-shopped, and finally, bad takes end up on the cutting room floor. The end result is what we see on the silver screen at the cinema. We leave the movie thinking that maybe Matt Damon is really Jason Bourne, that Scarlett Johansson is really the most beautiful, witty and knowledgeable person in Hollywood. Reality changes one's opinion.

In public, actors go through the ritual of trend setting. We envy the ugly-looking hats, boots, jeans, and swim suits that our heroes and heroines wear. We search out shops which sell like items. Well, some of us do. But, when we listen to some of these starlets speak without being prompted by their director, our heroes fall to Earth like junk from outer space. Yet we dwell on every word uttered by these programed individuals. Will we look forward to the next Oscar night? Not hardly.

Being born in a different century makes me miss my own childhood heroes. Clayton Moore and Jay Silverheels served as some of my most-admired characters. I still miss the orchestral rendition of the "William Tell Overture" and the hardy cry of "Hi, ho, Silver, Away!" The Lone Ranger would never have given a speech criticizing his own country for defeating a terrorist group. But, there is something we can question—those who answer the phone when we dial up a 1-800 number.

Ever had a problem with one of your multimedia products in the home? Difficulty interpreting your phone bill, cable subscription fees or Internet connections? When we encounter such troublesome things, we go to our working phones and dial up an 800 number listed under consumer services. If we are lucky, we get a local representative who might have attended public or private schools in our area. They might even speak English. However, since outsourcing services has taken place in almost every American company, the chances are good that you will be connected with someone in a Southeast Asian country.

Don't jump to conclusions. These people are good, hard-working individuals. They probably work 12-hour shifts, have no health insurance, no retirement package and they are usually courteous on the phone. However, English is not the first language of those who respond to our concerns. And, they are trained to ask survival-skill questions: "Yes, may I help you, sir? What is your name? What is your problem? And, yes, I will be able to help you." It is only when you begin to outline the specifics of your problem that a breakdown in communications takes place.

If you say, "How is your day going? I really need help on this one." The response you hear might be: "Yes, may I help you, sir? What is your name? What is your problem? And, yes, I will be able to help you." Now, the fun begins.

Not yet frustrated with your 1-800 correspondent, you realize Sgt. Friday's game rules must apply; "Only the facts, ma'am." Then you get to work trying to explain the source of your call. You might even get a formative answer. However, if you go astray and ask such things as, "When might I receive notification of my service?" Or, "How long will the repair take and when will I have my service restored?" This might be your answer: "Yes, may I help you, sir" "What is your name?" "What is your problem?" "And, yes, I will be able to help you." Rote learning was great in grade school, but conversations with 1-800 operators/ agents can lead to calls for Tylenol. But, a side bar to this problem is worse. Where is the American worker who should be taking your call?

American stockholders put pressure on the CEO's of their stock companies to cut costs and raise returns on their investments. American workers are laid off, services are outsourced, and yep, "Yes, may I help you, sir? What is your name...?" Ah, but the bulls are running strong on Wall Street.

Retirement, Socialization and Happy Hours

What is the secret to life? At the end of my visits to the local pharmacy, the place which dispenses all the little pills which keep me alive, the pharmaceutical worker gives me my prescriptions and usually says, "Is there anything else I can help you with?' My response is sometimes, "Could you tell me the secret to life?" More often than not, my pill dispenser smiles and offers something positive just to spur me on my way. But, it is the smile on the person's face which is important. People, at least the majority of them, are wonderful creatures. It has taken me years to acknowledge that.

Upon my retirement in 2001, depression set in. My thirty-seven year career in public school and university teaching was more than rewarding. It was, quite literally, lifesaving. Had I not chosen education, my path would have led back to OCS Quantico, and as a Marine officer, Vietnam would have taken its toll. In my career in schools, I was the first to arrive and the last to leave, and in the years in the classroom, I missed five days. Two of those days had to do with attendance at my mother's funeral; I liked what I did for a living. And, I had good reason to be pleased with my chosen profession.

My students, both in high school and at the university level, seemed to realize that their teacher liked what he was doing, and they appreciated the no-nonsense approach to teaching and learning they encountered in my classrooms. Leaving such an atmosphere was difficult, and it was important for me to set new goals and expectations if the rest of my life was going to go well. So, my wife and I invested in a small condo in Scottsdale, Arizona. It proved to be one of the best decisions we ever made.

There is something suspicious about newcomers to a living area. Who are these new people in our community?

Where do they come from? Do they have kids? Why are they here? My wife and I did not have to suffer any such inquisition; we were the first occupants in our new three-story building. We had the advantage of being the inquisitors and, more importantly, the greeters.

Our new condo was located on the first floor of our building which faces other two-story units called casitas. Our larger building is separated from the smaller units by an auto access lane and pedestrian walkway. That proved to be an advantage since passersby, dog walkers, joggers and other condo dwellers had to pass by our patio which opened up onto the thoroughfare. Our habit of taking our daily happy hour on our patio started something which made our decision to be escapees from northern winters more enjoyable than thought possible. It turned out to be life-extending.

My wife and I like people. Most human beings are gregarious although there is a tendency for individuals to approach strangers with caution. **Americans place an invisible bubble around them when in a strange place or when faced with those they don't know. That psychological shield can be penetrated if an acceptance of others is expressed. That's what my wife and I set out to do.**

Every afternoon, once chores, shopping and exercise was over for the day, my wife and I would end up on our patio where we had installed a little bar and stools. That's where we would review that day's activities and plan for the next. We would prepare some light hors-d'oeuvres, open a bottle of wine and retire to the outdoor patio area. Sitting at our little bar sipping either a red blend or a sauvignon blanc, we would watch the neighbors stroll by.

Whenever someone new to the area would pass our patio, we would always say hello or offer some kind of greeting having to do with the wonderful Arizona weather. We would often hear the recipients of our greeting say, "My, that looks good." Our response was always positive and usually included, "Stop by when you get a chance." Our new neighbors would smile and continue on their way, but at time passed, a few of our passersby would indeed stop by and introduce themselves. They were new, too, and they might not have had talkative neighbors back home where ever that was. Open hospitality and a smile go a long way to making friends.

There is a trend in America today, especially in more affluent areas of the country. More and more homeowners and renters have dogs. Our neighbors at Bella Vista, our community in Scottsdale, are no exception. Some of our neighbors have more than one dog. One of the first things my wife and I did was to make sure we had a good supply of mini milk-bone treats for our animal friends. The next thing we did was add to our bar stools on the patio. Garage sales and used-furniture outlets helped add needed seating on our patio, and the popularity of our "Only on days which end in D-A-Y" happy hours resulted in a big change; we needed more space for those who began to join us in our daily rituals on the patio.

Snow birds, those curious creatures like my wife and me who wanted to escape the rigors of northern winters, began leasing three-month long condo stays in our building. Chilly evenings and growing numbers of happy hour attendees forced us inside the building where a large meeting room was available. Once again, garage sales and used furniture outlets enabled us to collect a number of folding chairs and card tables. We are now able to accommodate over twenty persons at a time, and during Super Bowl Sunday and New Year's Eve, we have almost thirty attendees.

Everyone came to know exactly what BYOB meant, and most people show up with a small plate of hors-d'oeuvres to spike an appetite for dinner. Those same <u>tapas</u> serve to make tongues water and wag to the point where it is sometimes difficult to hear the person next to you. Some of us resort to sign language and facial gestures to make a point. If anything was indicative of social accord, it was the sound of multiple conversations taking place in what seemed like a New Orleans jazz concert where every instrument is playing a different rendition of the same theme. Coming out of all this joyous tumult was the organization of special events.

More snow birds at happy hours led to Super Bowl parties, New Year's Eve celebrations, birthday impromptus and pot-luck dinners. Such things punctuated the winter's calendar of events. In 2015, our December 31 get together had everyone taking part in a pajama party. Sleepwear of all kinds (all appropriate of course) supplied color, trends and various cuisine which enhanced our ringing in of the New Year. This year's festivities at the end of December will see a Hawaiian luau. Hawaiian shirts for the male contingent and the muumuu for the female should add even more color to our celebration. At times, religion does play a minor role.

One of our Jewish residents sponsored a get together celebrating Hanukkah. He made latkes potato pancakes for everyone. While that worked well, we do try to keep our playing field level, and religious celebrations are not encouraged. We do display a Christmas tree and we set up a menorah for our Jewish friends, and we do exchange verbal greetings in honor of our religious members. Too many true believers might offend those who profess other religions. So far, so good. Cohesion of the group is our special consideration, and it has served us well.

First of all, group members respect nationalities, allegiance to one's home country or state, and no one criticizes anyone else for being from the south, north, east or west. Whether one drinks red, white or rose wine, or chooses to have a bottled water or beer is never mentioned. In our group, we have vegans, meat eaters and those who shun shellfish. No one in our group has ever produced a cigarette or cigar. Peer pressure is silent but evident. Our Canadian, Hispanic and other happy hour- practitioners are all welcome. Wouldn't it be a great thing if happy hours took place in the Middle East?

Will our little gatherings continue? Probably, at least until we forget about our silent pledge to refrain from discussing religion or political affiliation. Besides, our luau is coming up, and the secret to life might just be this simple---live it.

Twinkle, Twinkle Little Star; the Planets and God's Creations

You do not have to possess the insight of Stephen Hawking to behold and appreciate the world and its surrounding universe. No telescopes are necessary for you to marvel at what a night sky offers up in the way of nature's beauty. The waxing and waning of our moon bathed in the sun's light radiating from the other side of the Earth sends romantic signals to humans and animals alike. Our ancestors worshiped such things, and in our own way, we still do. There are other things up there, too.

Vincent Van Gogh was so inspired by nature's offerings that he gave us "Starry, Starry Night". Our own sightings of distant suns conjure up all sorts of thoughts which range from the contemplation of the constellations to the making of a wish at the sighting of an evening's first star. That sparkle, that wonderment of white on black plays a magical tune on the strings of our mind and heart. And, all this, this wide expanse of space is crisscrossed with the flickering of the airliners' lights which blink on and off thousands of feet above our heads. Awesome! Then, our mighty sun transforms our beautiful backdrop and turns night into day.

Daylight, that wonderful panorama of light and color, offers us some magnificent views. Here in the Arizona desert, winter is morphing into spring and summer. Little lizards of all sizes and shapes scurry to and fro like some bursting fireworks bouncing among the sand and rocks. These little reptiles search for some small bug which will sustain life for them. Other larger species of reptiles slither about. They carry an ominous beauty, but some things are better left untouched. And one does not have to move far away from their living area to take in the spectacle of nature around them.

Wild peccary, more commonly called javelina, coyotes, rabbits, hummingbirds, ground squirrels, mourning doves and speckled woodpeckers abound in this wonderland of fauna. Along with the giant saguaro, the ocotillo, the cholla, and the beavertail cactus, God has painted a wonderful landscape for our enjoyment. Eat your heart out, Vincent; if we take the time, we can paint a masterpiece every day.

My son and daughter offer some good examples of those who take pleasure in life. Since he was a little boy, my son has had a dog in his life. In every case, he has shown a respect for the animals he has owned. My thoughts on this can be summarized in this sentence: At a young age, those who show cruelty toward animals usually spend some time in prison. Kindness, consideration and care are watchwords my son uses with his pets. And, a deep-down remorse takes place whenever my son crosses the line or inadvertently harms an animal.

One day at home, after complaining to my son about pigeons which had a nasty habit of creating a mess near our pool deck, he wanted to help his father solve the problem. A pellet gun was used to bring down one of those winged innocent things to Earth. Almost immediately, my son expressed regret for what he had done. He had taken a life. Since that time, he has never fired a shot at any animal. But, he did complete a four-year enlistment in the United States Marine Corps.

My daughter has similar qualities. She extends the love she has for children to all the animals around her. She is a day-care giver for children of parents who teach in the area schools. Doing so allows her the same vacations her own children enjoy. Her home is surrounded with bird feeders, bird baths, and in winter, the bird baths are heated. Rabbits, groundhogs, squirrels, chipmunks and deer parade through her lawn gathering up seeds she has spread for nature's creatures. She sometimes talks to these little animals. No, she is neither a Dr. Doolittle nor psychotic. She loves life and she loves nature. The sight and thought that I place on watching the tolerance and kindness of my own children toward people and things is just another pleasure I take in this life. And, yes, I thank God for giving me the opportunity to observe all this.

<u>Carpe diem.</u> If we were to take time to observe the things and people around us---friends, strangers, and family, depression would be a thing of the past.

Let me end this rambling on a happy note. Let me tell you about the nose.

A Nose by any other name...

My honors high-school French classes had just finished a unit of study on Edmond Rostand's classic play, <u>Cyrano de Bergerac.</u> My students, all seniors, were completing their sixth year of study of their target language, and they found the seventeenth-century hero, Cyrano, to be impressive. They had read the play in French, memorized some of the well-known scenes including the famous "Tirade du Nez" portrayed so well in the film based on this masterpiece by the actor, Gerard Depardieu. We watched the film is class. The students were mesmerized by the fantastic authenticity of scenery depicted in the film. But, more importantly, the students learned that physical beauty is not the most cherished characteristic of a person's physiognomy. By this time, television specials on Rostand's play and Steve Martin's portrayal of his character have allowed most of us to realize that Cyrano's oversize proboscis is the object on which we focus. Such recognition came well before American service men and women were coming home from Iraq and Afghanistan disfigured by the evils of war, and perhaps made those in my class more appreciative of the sacrifices their fellow Americans had made. Cyrano would have been proud of today's heroes, and something tells me that my students who had studied the concept of passion of the heart would also equate twenty-first century heroes with those of the seventeenth. Returning home from school one evening, I decided that more time should be devoted to my grandson Mackinley. He was young enough to learn the lessons just taught and portrayed in the above film.

"Mackey", the more informal and familiar name, was that used to refer to, call, and address my grandson. At the tender age of two and a half, Mackey was already reading from children's books on a second-grade level. Mackey's mother had read to him while he was still in the womb, and whether such things take root before birth is now a subject of much discussion in our country. In any event, Mackey was a reader, and my desire to inspire him with the humanity portrayed in Rostand's play was still fresh in my mind. Using a little technique which had worked in my French classes, I encouraged Mackey to watch a film with me. The original film done by Depardieu might have been too much for my now three-year old grandson. So, I decided that instead of the French-language film, we would watch the American comparative film---<u>Roxanne.</u>

Yes, subtitles were available on the French version, but my thoughts centered on the film in which Steve Martin (yep, the banjo guy) did an admirable case of comparative literature in the American film. The antics, verbal innuendoes and character impersonations made by Martin pleased my grandson. We discussed the reasons for the actor's feelings of rejection and dismay, and my new little learner seemed to fully assimilate what I had hoped to teach. But, a little boy's focus does not always center on the lessons of the French classics for long periods of time, and I had to move on to other things which might interest him. Mackey's mother served to let us focus on other things.

Mackey was soon going to have a little sister. Days went by, and we all waited impatiently for the blessed event to take place. Finally, my daughter was rushed to the hospital escorted by her husband and my wife. The job given me was babysitter to Mackey, and the two of us did what was expected of us until we were called to the hospital. Mackey was going to have a little sister.

So, off we go, the two of us, proud grandparent and little brother, to the hospital. One the way, I tried to explain that a wonderful gift had been offered; Mackey was to have a loving companion in his home while growing up. Things would be shared, events and outings would be appreciated together, and a close friend and supporter would always be nearby. Such things seem to slip off the tongue by grandfathers who recognize miracles.

Mackey and I did what most adoring family members do when seeing a new-born part of the family. We cooed, babbled and verbally splashed congratulatory greetings over mother and child. Everyone agreed that the new-born baby was the most beautiful thing we had ever seen. We exclaimed that she was destined for the most fantastic achievements in her life ahead. An angel had been born in front of our very eyes. That being done, it was now my duty to take Mackey back home and prepare lunch. So, we headed out.

We had almost reached the exit door of the hospital leading to the parking lot when all I had taught Mackey about the French classics and tolerance came crashing to the ground like some building brought town by an earthquake.

Walking toward us dressed in hospital scrubs and with a stethoscope wrapped around his neck was, most assuredly, one of the hospital's physicians. But, the man's olfactory was beyond description. Steve Martin would have stuttered. Cyrano would have thought himself handsome. The thing was huge. My efforts to turn back toward Mackey's mother's room were thwarted by the little guy that I had in tow, and he was focused on the man's nose like some radar-guided missile heading toward a target.

The doctor, a person of South-East Asian descent, had one outstanding physical deformity. Square in the middle of his face was the biggest snout I had ever seen. My grandson's gaze hadn't changed. His eyes were locked on the thing coming toward him. I felt my grandson's hand close in mine, and I knew then that there was no turning back. My inner voice uttered, "No, Mackey, no!" It was too late.

The doctor, God bless him, carried a big smile underneath this living appendage above his lips. He said, "Hi, little boy.

How are you today?" Mackey looked up at the amazing thing holding court on the man's face, and with his index finger extended toward his sighted objective like some super telescope seeking out new worlds, he said, "Poppy, look at that nose!" I was devastated. I smiled at the physician's greeting and said something in return while dragging a mesmerized little boy toward the exit. Still focused on the thing which had drawn his attention, Mackey was reluctant to leave such a sight behind. Approaching our car, my only recourse was to say, "Mackey, how about some ice cream."

Sharia Law: A Primer

This last piece has questionable sources. There is not a lot I know on this subject, but it is, considering the events taking place, something we should all look into. World War II had a devastating effect on this world. Millions upon millions of people lost their lives. Evil empires and warlords were erased from the face of the Earth and baby booms took place in almost every country. But, something else occurred which had an influence on the 21st century. Great Britain and France lost hold of their overseas territories.

Since 1947, Britain lost overseas colonies in the Middle East and in Africa. French North African colonies revolted and both France and Britain, crippled by war debts, could not hold onto their overseas territories. Syria, Iraq, Iran, Afghanistan, Algeria, Libya and the Congo won a short-lived freedom. And, in the vacuum produced by a European pullout, something ominous was to take its place---the growth of Islam and sharia law.

This short treatise is by no means a definitive explanation of Islamic law. It is for my own benefit that any research took place. More is needed. The following are just a few minor facts which came to light on the subject.

Sharia law is the legal base for life as it applies to Muslims. It has at its base two main sources---the alleged life, actions and words of Muhammad called <u>Sunnah</u>, and the Muslim holy book, the <u>Quran</u>, supposedly authored by Muhammad. Any interpretation of sharia law is called, "figh" and imams, so-called blood-line relatives of Muhammad, have full reign of these interpretations.

The law itself, sharia, comes from the Arabic word denoting "path to the water hole" which, when one considers life in the arid desert environment, is understandable. Those devoted to Islam believe that following the examples of

Muhammad's life comes only second after the writings in the <u>Quran.</u> I took the time to read the book twice. That was enough.

As in Christianity, many sects make up the Muslim faith. We are most familiar with Sunni and Shia, the two largest denominations Islam. Both sects believe that the other is advocating the wrong path to the water hole, and they are willing to die for their belief. Such an attitude leads to bombs being exploded in crowded market places. But, all Muslims are expected to adhere to the basic tenets of sharia. By doing so, you will pray five times daily, observe fasting, practice the articles of faith as set down in the <u>Quran,</u> obey obligatory giving of charity or tax and make the pilgrimage, the hajj to Mecca, the birthplace of Muhammad. So far, so good. But, when it comes to women, those who profess there to be a "war on women" in America should step back and take a look at Islam and sharia law.

In court cases, there are usually no lawyers. Trials are conducted by a judge. There is no jury system, no cross examination of witnesses, and male witnesses are considered more reliable than female witnesses. In civil cases, in most Islamic countries, a Muslim woman witness is considered half the worth and reliability than a man. Ah, but there is more.

A woman's inheritance in family matters is unequal and less than a man's. Sharia authorizes the institution of slavery (Louis Farrakhan, where are you?). And, under Islamic law, Muslim men could have sexual relations with female captives and slaves. Remember the young American woman captured in Syria?

It is impossible for me to outline everything about sharia law. But, let's take a look at a listing of a few of the intolerances of Islamic law. Theft is punishable by amputation of the right hand. Criticizing or denying any part of the Quran is punishable by death.

Criticizing Allah, the moon god of Islam or drawing a picture of Muhammad is punishable by death. Remember <u>Charlie Hebdo?</u> A Muslim man can marry an infant girl and consummate the marriage by the age of 9. A woman can have one husband, a man can have up to 4 wives. Muhammad, should he return, can have more than four. A man can beat his wife for insubordination. There is a running joke among Muslim men which states, "If you do not know why you beat your wife, she will." Yes, there is more. But, the rest is up to you.

As for me, give me the American Constitution. The boys from the original thirteen colonies did a good job. God bless America.

A Wall or Ellis Island Southwest?

Politicians, so-called liberals and conservatives, and Americans concerned with their economic future, discuss building a wall across the entire southwestern border of the United States. Stemming the flow of illegal aliens (oops, undocumented aliens) is on the minds of millions of Americans whose lives might be affected by the ever-increasing multitudes of people wishing to enter the land of plenty. Is such a concern justified?

If you are an American taxpayer, growing school populations without a secure tax base could be disconcerting. The difficulty of educating young children whose language is other than English causes elementary school teachers to wonder how they will cope with mandates presented before them by the federal government. Is a wall across the southern border of the United States the answer?

The cost of building such a wall would be astronomical. And, building such a thing would most assuredly morally contaminate the reputation America has presented to others across the world. Our Statue of Liberty holds in her hands a plaque which reads, "Give me your tired, your poor..." So, is there an alternative? Certainly. Back to the future; build an Ellis Island-like institution in the Southwest and offer a welcoming hand to future Americans. Hey, we did it before, and this is how it worked.

Ellis Island was established in 1892, and was in operation until 1954. Twelve million immigrants (including Bob Hope) passed through this busiest immigrant inspection station. But, the most-important word in this last sentence was, "inspection". Take a look at what was done at Ellis Island in the way of making sure that newcomers to the United States would not become a burden to their new country.

New arrivals to the U.S. were asked 29 questions including name, occupation and the amount of money they carried (between 18 and 20 dollars was expected of immigrants). This last item was important because the U.S. wanted immigrants to be able to support themselves and have money to get started---something which is not required today. Unfortunately, welfare steps its heavy foot down, and newcomers are more and more reluctant to do for themselves. But, there is more.

Before 1954, those with visible health problems or disease were sent home or held in the island's hospital facilities for long periods of time. Unskilled workers were rejected because they were "likely to become a public charge". About 2 percent were denied admission to the U.S. and sent back to their country of origin for reasons such as being a chronic contagious disease case, criminal background or insanity. No such vetting is taking place with those who enter our country illegally today.

And, with "sanctuary cities" protecting illegal aliens today, the U.S. government is unable or unwilling to cope with the problem.

So, instead of building a wall, let us build an Ellis Island in the Southwest of the United States. We would be more able to welcome those who want to become Americans and contribute to the continuous rise of our way of life. But, let us not forget that we will continue to have those who will say, "What do you mean by asking such questions? I have my rights." That depends on who might be asking the questions. Just build it.

Envoi

Ah, Prince, take not a bitter view
Of opinions in front of you.
Time will tell whether they will last.
But, the fact that they have been cast
Makes the mind think
they might ring true.

Nothing mentioned means nothing due.
Better mouthed than held in review.
If all these words seem hard and fast,
Things here taken as a repast
Makes the mind think
they might ring true.

About the Author

 Allen R. Remaley loves his family and the life granted him. He loves his country and served four years as an enlisted United States Marine. He questions his Good Conduct Medal by saying, "How could a mean, lean, green Marine earn a medal like that?" After his military service, he attended colleges and universities in this country and abroad, and at the age of fifty-eight, completed his doctorate in French. He can make mistakes in four languages. Among his hobbies are playing pickle ball, strumming an old banjo, enjoying happy hours with his wife and with his friends, contemplating the miracle of life, and on occasion, he will write something down thinking that he is the first to have done so. How bizarre. He and his wife make their home in Saratoga Springs, New York and in Scottsdale, Arizona.

 Scottsdale, Arizona
 April 23, 2016

Printed in the United States
By Bookmasters